Y is for Yellowhammer
An Alabama Alphabet

Written by Carol Crane and Illustrated by Ted Burn

Sleeping Bear Press™

2395 South Huron Parkway, Ste. 200
Ann Arbor, MI 48104
www.sleepingbearpress.com

Printed and bound in the United States.

10 9 8 7 6

Library of Congress Cataloging-in-Publication Data
Crane, Carol, 1933-
Y is for yellowhammer : an Alabama alphabet / by Carol Crane ;
illustrated by Ted Burn.
p. cm.
Summary: Presents information about the state of Alabama
in an alphabetical arrangement.
ISBN 978-1-58536-118-2
1. Alabama-Juvenile literature. 2. English language-Alphabet-Juvenile
literature. [1. Alabama. 2. Alphabet.] I. Burn, Ted, 1940- ill. II. Title.
F326.3 .C73 2003
975.7—dc21   2003010380

*To Dr. MaryAnn Manning and friends at UAB, to my sister Beth
and Roger Johnston, who lived in Alabama for seventeen years,
to Ann Vest, a great educator, and Cookie and Paul, Roll Tide fans.*

CAROL

❧

*To my loving and patient wife Dianne, and to the very
helpful and patient staff at Sleeping Bear Press.*

TED

When in 1939 the seal of Alabama was approved, the senate and house of representatives all agreed that the state's most important feature was its rivers. It is the only state to show the outline of the state and its important rivers on the great seal. The first explorers, the Native Americans, the pioneers, and later the industrialists used the rivers for transportation and growth.

The Alabama River and the Tombigbee, the longest rivers in Alabama, meet and form the Mobile River which flows into the Gulf of Mexico. Other important rivers are the Chattahoochee, Cahaba, Black Warrior, Coosa, and the Choctawhatchee.

There are no natural lakes in Alabama. On some of the rivers, hydroelectric dams were built. The backwaters of these dams turned hundreds of miles of rushing water into acres of lakes.

A is for Alabama's amazing rivers,
Cahaba, Black Warrior, and Tennessee too.
They're so important the official state seal shows
Alabama waterways in review.

I walk among the many colored blossoms,
seeing flittering butterflies and birds as I roam.
This once quaint riverfront fishing camp
stands for **B**, the Bellingrath Gardens and home.

Bb

Walter Bellingrath and his wife Bessie bought riverfront land to use as a fishing camp more than 70 years ago. The land was like a jungle but the couple worked hard for many years to grow gardens in the perfect Alabama climate. Today you can see beautiful flowers 12 months out of the year, including the state flower, the camellia, and the official wildflower, the oak leaf hydrangea. The camellia belongs to the tea family and has been known to live hundreds of years. The oak leaf hydrangea was first recorded in the 1770s.

Butterfly gardens at Bellingrath attract the monarch butterfly, the state insect, and the eastern tiger swallowtail, which has been recognized as the state butterfly and mascot. The southern longleaf pine is the state tree and is called a "late bloomer," as it grows very little above the ground during its first 10 years.

C is for the many Caves and Caverns,
    magnificent and beautiful formations;
DeSoto, Sequoyah, and Russell to name a few,
    known as the oldest in the nation.

DeSoto Cave, near Childersburg, Alabama was first recorded in 1796. It was named after the Spanish explorer Hernando DeSoto, who discovered the cave in 1540. Inside the cave, onyx, a colorful semiprecious stone, was found. Today, it is called DeSoto Caverns Park.

The Sequoyah Caverns have smooth walkways through colored formations and looking glass pools. Here names, initials, and dates going back to 1824 have been found on the cave walls.

Russell Cave became the refuge for Indians over 10,000 years ago. Native Americans inhabited many of the caves during the winter months.

D stands for Dixie,
    all Alabamians have great pride in.
Our state is "The Heart of Dixie,"
        a heritage passed from kin to kin.

Before the Civil War (1861-1865), Louisiana issued $10 notes that were used as money. The notes had the French word "dix" on them, which means 10. This led the South to be known as Dixieland. Alabama was the capital of the Confederacy during the Civil War so it became known as the "Heart of Dixie."

Alabama is bordered on the west by Mississippi, to the north by Tennessee, on the east by Georgia, and by Florida to the south.

E e

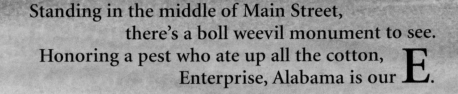

Standing in the middle of Main Street,
 there's a boll weevil monument to see.
Honoring a pest who ate up all the cotton,
 Enterprise, Alabama is our E.

In the 1800s cotton was the main crop of Alabama. Then an evil weevil, the Mexican boll weevil, found its way into the state and destroyed most of the cotton crops. The growers of the area decided to honor this pesky insect with a monument, because it forced them to grow other crops. At the base of the monument are the words:

In profound appreciation of the boll weevil and what it has done as the herald of prosperity, this monument was erected by the citizens of Enterprise, Coffee County, Alabama.

Today Alabama still grows cotton, but its main crop is peanuts. The pecan was officially designated as the state nut in 1982.

When summer is over and fall leaves turn to crimson red, football season starts for Alabama fans. The stadiums are crowded with young and old coming to cheer on their favorite teams. Records have been set in bowl game wins, players have gone on to new careers, and fans have loved to relive the history of their favorite play.

Young Paul "Bear" Bryant got his nickname for wrestling a bear. This poor farm boy grew up to be one of the most honored legends in University of Alabama's coaching history. His trademark was his checkered hat and the saying, "If you believe in yourself and have pride and never quit, you'll be a winner."

"Roll Tide" is the cheer on everyone's lips at the University of Alabama in Tuscaloosa. "War Eagle" is the chant from Auburn University.

The Heisman Trophy, given to the most outstanding college football player, honors John William Heisman, former football coach at Auburn University. Both universities started playing the game of football in 1892.

Ff

F stands for Football Fans,
　　　you can hear the crowds roar and cheer!
"Roll Tide," "War Eagle," and the legend Bear Bryant;
　　　young and old come from far and near.

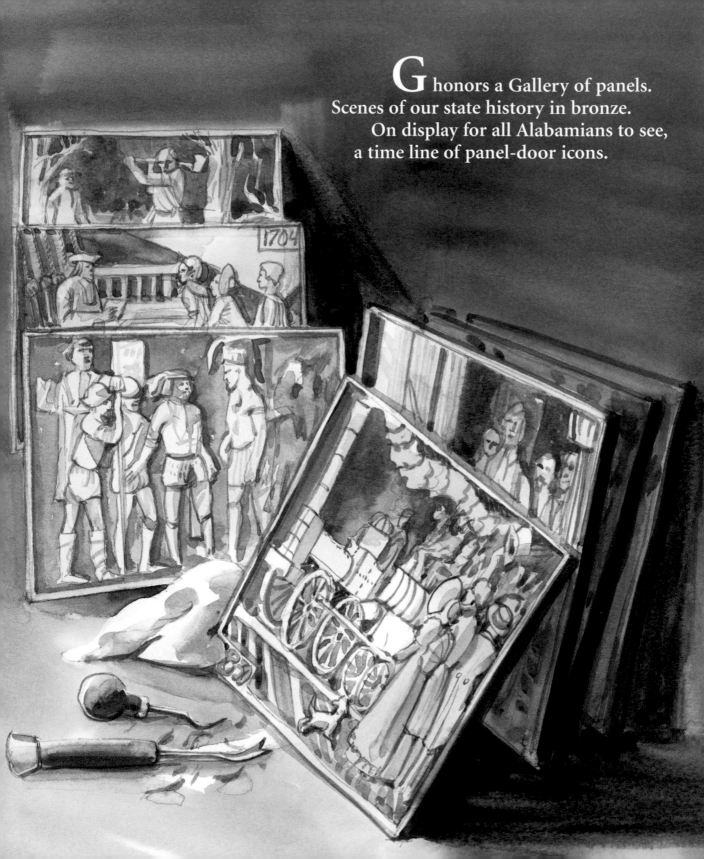

G honors a Gallery of panels.
Scenes of our state history in bronze.
On display for all Alabamians to see,
a time line of panel-door icons.

Nathan H. Glick, a native of Birmingham, Alabama and later schooled in Montgomery, was chosen in 1940 to design bronze doors for the Alabama Department of Archives and History that illustrate the time line of Alabama history. Later, the doors were placed inside.

The panels depict Alabama history from the "Meeting of DeSoto and Chief Tuscaloosa" through the "First Railroad in Alabama," and the final panel, which honors the state's gratitude to all Alabamians who fought in World War I.

Gg

H h

Hank Aaron is our **H**,
a baseball player who made us proud.
When the bat hit the ball,
you could hear the roar of the crowd.

Henry Louis Aaron was born in Mobile, Alabama in 1934. During 23 seasons in the major leagues, his record shows him to be one of the greatest hitters in the game of baseball. He was named the National League's Most Valuable Player and led the Braves to win the 1957 World Series. He was elected to the Baseball Hall of Fame in 1982.

Many other famous athletes can call Alabama home. Some of them are: Carl Lewis, track athlete; Joe Louis, boxer; Willie Mays, baseball player; and Joe Namath, football player. Jesse Owens of the United States was the hero of the 1936 Summer Olympic Games. He won four gold medals in track and field. He worked hard to teach clean living, fair play, and patriotism.

Helen Keller was born in 1880 at her family homestead, Ivy Green. When she was 19 months old, she became very ill. Afterward, her mother discovered that she was both blind and deaf as a result of the illness. As Helen grew she became unmanageable, and a teacher was hired to try to teach her to understand through the sense of touch. The teacher's name was Anne Sullivan.

It took some time and a lot of hard work, but one day Helen held her hand under the water pump and connected water with the letters her teacher wrote in her hand. Today in Tuscumbia, Alabama at Ivy Green, the home of Helen Keller, a very famous play, "The Miracle Worker," is performed at an outdoor theater.

Alabama was the 22nd state admitted to the Union. The 22nd quarter released in the United States state quarter program has saluted Helen Keller. The first U.S. coin in circulation to include braille, Keller's name appears on the coin in both English and braille. The quarter, which includes the slogan "Spirit of Courage," shows Keller reading a book in braille.

Ii

Here at the birthplace of Helen Keller,
where the "Miracle Worker" is seen.
America's "First Lady of Courage,"
I is our letter for Ivy Green.

During the early morning hours, this natural phenomenon may occur and last for two hours. Scientists think oxygen is depleted, sending marine life to the surface of the water and the shore. Whenever this happens on the eastern shore of Mobile Bay, visitors and locals alike have buckets in hand and run to the water's edge, scooping up seafood when the call of "Jubilee!" is heard.

During other times, vacationers may stroll the beach and find many different shells. The official shell of Alabama is the Johnstone's Junonia, a peachy cream base color tinged with bright yellow. This shell is only found in Alabama. However, it is rare to find one on the shore because this mollusk lives in deep offshore waters.

In 1955, the Fighting Tarpon was named the saltwater fish of Alabama.

J j

J is for the shout of "Jubilee!"
  With buckets we run to the bay.
Scooping up flounder, shrimp, and crabs,
  a seafood lover's holiday!

K k

K stands for Kymulga Bridge,
one of many old bridges in our state.
There is also a gristmill,
where corn can be ground while you wait.

There are many old covered bridges in Alabama. Pioneers and settlers needed a way to get across rivers and valleys, so wooden bridges were made. The Kymulga Bridge was built in 1861. The gristmill was built during the Civil War. The huge wheel that goes round and round uses five sets of grinding rocks. Ground corn is used to make grits, hush puppies, and corn dressing at Thanksgiving time.

The eastern wild turkey is the state game bird of Alabama.

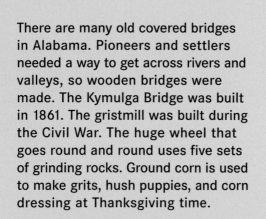

Landmark Park is near Dothan, Alabama, located in the wire grass region of southeast Alabama. Here we can experience what it was like living on a farm in the 1890s. At this living history farm you will be greeted by sheep, goats, pigs, chickens, cows, and a mule. You will see what it was like to go to school in a one-room schoolhouse. There is a pioneer log cabin, smokehouse, cane mill syrup shed, and a blacksmith shop. This area is along the Chattahoochee Trace. The word trace means road. The settlers worked hard to plant and grow crops in this large stretch of land that was covered with wire grass. Wire grass is clumps of stiff, dry grass.

L l

L stands for Landmark Park,
a living historical farm.
The official Alabama Agricultural Museum,
that old pioneer homestead charm.

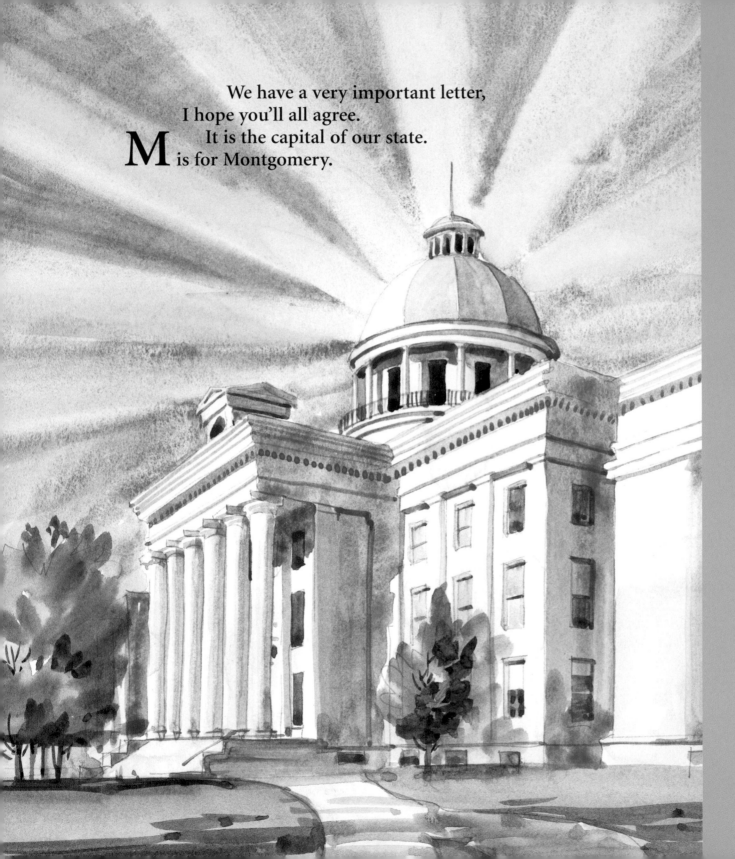

We have a very important letter,
I hope you'll all agree.
It is the capital of our state.
M is for Montgomery.

Montgomery, the capital of Alabama, was named for General Richard Montgomery, a Revolutionary War hero. It was officially named the capital city in 1846. Located on the Alabama River in the rich black belt region, it quickly became the center of cotton plantations. It is also one of the largest livestock and dairy centers in the southeast. The area around the capitol building has often been called Goat Hill because at one time, goats grazed on the site where it stands. The current state flag was adopted in 1895. It has a crimson cross of St. Andrew on a field of white.

Alabama is the site of a number of firsts. It was among the first states to secede from the Union at the beginning of the Civil War. In 1886 the world's first electric trolley system was introduced in Montgomery. In 1965 a famous 50-mile walk from Selma to Montgomery took place to ensure civil rights for all Americans.

Now, N stands for the Night "Stars Fell on Alabama,"
falling and shooting stars flashed through the skies.
November 12, 1833 was the night,
meteors so bright it dazzled the eyes.

When you see a meteor, it seems to shoot quickly across the sky. A meteor is rock and debris called meteoroids that are burning high in the Earth's upper atmosphere. They travel at thousands of miles an hour. They quickly ignite 30 to 80 miles above the ground. Their small size and great brightness might make you think it is a star. If you see the meteor fall all the way to the ground, it's easy to think you just saw a star fall.

In Alabama in 1833, people began to see a few of these falling stars. However, a few hours later, the few meteors turned into tens of thousands. Some of the meteors ended in fireballs and left smoke trails that lasted for 20 minutes. Years later, a song was published and is still popular today. It is called "Stars Fell on Alabama." Across the top of the Alabama license plate are falling stars.

n
N

This eight-sided house was built between 1859 and 1861. It is located in the unique little town of Clayton, Alabama. It has been placed on the National Register of Historic Places and is the only antebellum octagonal house in Alabama. Four chimneys rise up into a cupola and enclose the staircase of this eight-sided structure. On the main floor, four large rooms, two small rooms, and two hallways open up onto the porch. There is a wraparound porch where in the summer, lemonade would be served on hot days.

O is for an Octagonal House,
Alabama's only eight-sided house.
Round and round the poor cat chasing,
and never catching the mouse.

Rosa Parks was born in Montgomery, Alabama in 1913. Rosa's mother was a schoolteacher and taught her daughter until she was 11. Then Rosa went to the Industrial School for Girls. Later she also attended Alabama State College. Today she is known as "the mother of the civil rights movement."

It was late December and Rosa was tired from working all day. She found a seat on a bus to carry her home, but a white man boarded the bus and demanded Rosa move to the back. She refused to do so. She was put in jail for this. Today, as a senior citizen, she is still concerned about freedom, equality, and justice for all people.

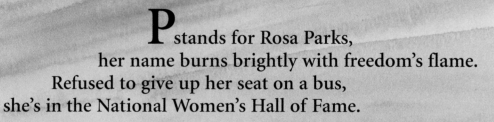

P stands for Rosa Parks,
her name burns brightly with freedom's flame.
Refused to give up her seat on a bus,
she's in the National Women's Hall of Fame.

In 1997 the Pine Burr Quilt became the official state quilt. The Freedom Quilting Bee grew out of the Civil Rights Movement. Many local people lost work, their farms, and their homes because they registered to vote. The women used their sewing skills to earn family income. At first, quilts were hung out on clotheslines to sell. Now, the Freedom Bee company is the largest employer in Alberta, Alabama where quilts, potholders, placemats, and napkins are made.

Birmingham, Alabama has a six-block tribute to the Civil Rights Movement. Here you may visit the Birmingham Civil Rights Institute, Kelly Ingram Park, Alabama Jazz Hall of Fame, Sixteenth Street Baptist Church, and the Fourth Avenue Business District. All of these historical exhibitions tell the history of the African-American life and the struggle for civil rights.

Q is for Pine Burr Quilt,
a pattern of hundreds of stitches.
It is Alabama's official state quilt,
unfolding colors of beautiful riches.

Rr

R is our Red Bellied Turtle,
the official Alabama reptile.
Basking in the noonday sun,
enjoying the Mobile delta lifestyle.

The Alabama red bellied turtle loves the Mobile delta. It is here in the delta, where rivers meet the ocean, that the turtle is seen sunning himself on logs. Rivers carry soil and dirt, and new land is formed. This new, soil-rich land is known as a delta. The water is either fresh or brackish, which means a mix of salt and freshwater. This turtle is found nowhere else in the world.

The Red Hills salamander was named the official amphibian of Alabama in 2000. This small salamander is on the endangered list as the natural home of the salamander is threatened.

The Shoals area is often called Muscle Shoals. The Shoals are a series of rapids and falls along the Tennessee River tamed by dams. Many varieties of freshwater mussels are found here. Have you ever been served a plate of mussels?

In Tuscumbia, a coon dog cemetery honors many faithful friends. Pumpkin farms with huge pumpkins are grown in this area. A small part of the Natchez Trace Parkway, where Davy Crockett first explored our country, runs through the Shoals. The Dismals Canyon is undisturbed wilderness with seven natural bridges formed by scenic rock.

The northwest corner of Alabama is known for many historical places to visit. The Alabama Music Hall of Fame is located in Tuscumbia. Many famous musicians record their music here. W.C. Handy Home and Museum, the home of the "Father of the Blues," is in Florence, Alabama.

S stands for the Shoals,
with so many places to explore.
A coon dog cemetery, canyons and bridges,
music, farms, parks, and more.

Washington and Carver,
two great men in history.
A founder, an inventor,
Tuskegee is our T.

Booker Taliaferro Washington was born a slave. George Washington Carver was also born a slave. These two men left a legacy for all mankind. Booker T. Washington founded Tuskegee Institute, one of Alabama's first schools for the training of African-American teachers. The school started with 30 students. The students built the buildings brick by brick. Now there are more than 160 buildings on many acres of land. Tuskegee soon became one of the nation's most important African-American educational institutions, and Booker T. Washington became one of the nation's most influential African-American leaders.

In 1896, Booker T. Washington brought the African-American scientist George Washington Carver to Tuskegee to serve as the institute's director of agricultural research. He worked for 50 years and developed hundreds of uses for peanuts (including peanut butter!), sweet potatoes, and soybeans.

Tt

U u

Battleship *USS Alabama* is our U,
moored in the port city of Mobile.
This very important Alabama city
has so much history to reveal.

Mobile is the only seaport in Alabama. It was founded in 1702 by explorer Jean Baptiste le Moyne. Many countries wanted this valuable area, as it was the gateway to new land and rivers. Fort Gaines on Dauphine Island and Fort Morgan were guards to the entrance of Mobile Bay during the Civil War.

Today Mobile is the home of shipyards where you can still see ships being built. It is here, on the bay, that the battleship *USS Alabama* is moored and honored in Memorial Park. Mobile Bay is the second largest natural gas reserve in the world.

The city of Mobile is known as the Azalea City. In 1754 Fifise Langlois brought these bright pink blossoms here from his father's garden in Toulouse, France. Today, everywhere you look you see azaleas in bloom! In fact, there are 50 varieties of colors.

In 1704 the original Mardi Gras was celebrated in Mobile.

The statue, Vulcan, was cast in 1904 as Birmingham, Alabama's entry to the St. Louis World Fair. It was first displayed there as a tribute to the steel industry. It is the largest cast-iron statue in the world. It stands 56 feet high and weighs approximately 103,000 pounds. It stands on a pedestal atop Red Mountain and over-looks the largest city in Alabama.

V stands for Vulcan,
a cast-iron statue tribute.
A symbol of the iron and steel industry,
a true "Magic City" salute.

Wilson Dam was named after President Woodrow Wilson. It is a mile long. You can drive over the top of it and see boat and barge traffic going through the locks. This lock is one of the highest lifts in the world. At one time, the river was very dangerous with rapids and jagged rocks that wrecked many boats. The TVA, or Tennessee Valley Authority, built a series of dams in the 1930s to make the river safer for transportation. There are other dams on the Tennessee River, including the Wheeler, Guntersville, Pickwick, and Nickajack Dams.

You may see many fishing boats in the rivers of Alabama. Sports fishermen are trying to catch the state's freshwater fish, the largemouth bass.

Our **W** is the Wilson and Wheeler Locks,
where boats are lowered and raised on the river.
There is also a dam where you can watch
captains steering barges with goods to deliver.

X is for the X-15A-2 rocket,
it gave the space program a start.
Once on display at Huntsville,
this space center played a big part.

The U.S. Space and Rocket Center is the largest hands-on space museum in the world. It is located in Huntsville, Alabama. You may want to sign up and go to space camp where all the thrills of going on a trip into space can be experienced!

Near by are the George C. Marshall Space Flight Center and the Redstone Arsenal. It is here that scientist Dr. Wernher von Braun developed the early rockets that launched America's first satellites and carried the first astronauts into space. The X-15A-2 rocket can be seen at the space center.

"X" stands for experimental, and this was one of the first manned rockets. The Saturn rockets took man to the moon. It also took the giant space station Skylab into space, where it orbited the earth. The space buggy Lunar Rover was also built here.

Y y

The Yellowhammer is also called the Common Flicker. The undersides of the wings and tail are bright yellow. The male is a gray-brown color and is often found in cities as well as in the country. Yellowhammers are reported to eat more ants than any other American bird. It was made the official state bird in 1927.

Alabama has been known as the "Yellowhammer State" since the Civil War. The soldiers of Huntsville, Alabama wore fine, new uniforms of gray with bits of brilliant yellow cloth on their sleeves, collars, and coattails. When they arrived in Hopkinsville, Kentucky and rode past the soldiers there, someone yelled out, "Yellowhammer, Yellowhammer, flicker, flicker!" The name spread throughout the Confederate Army and all Alabama troops were referred to as the Yellowhammers.

Our official state bird's name,
history does glorify.
The uniforms of the Civil War soldiers,
Yellowhammer is our Y.

Brother Joseph Zoettl came to America from Bavaria at the age of 14. He came to Saint Bernard Abbey in 1892, the first and only Benedictine Abbey in Alabama. He worked 40 years building miniature reproductions of famous churches, shrines, and buildings from all over the world. He used marbles, jars, limestone, shells, and even a discarded birdcage, which is the "dome" of his St. Peter's Basilica. The Hanging Gardens of Babylon, ancient Jerusalem, and Rome's Pantheon are just a few of the remarkable works of this creative man. Today, parents and children can see many wonders of the world on three acres of land.

Z stands for Brother Joseph Zoettl
creating 125 buildings to show.
He worked for 40 years
on the Ave Maria Grotto.

Cotton Picking Questions

1. Where are the Looking Glass Lakes located?

2. What famous Indian chief was described as being 7 feet tall and had a city named after him?

3. What is the Alabama state motto?

4. What river is a waterway for barges?

5. On December 14, 1819 Alabama became the 22nd state in the Union. Which president signed into law the resolution that admitted Alabama into the Union?

6. What is the official American Folk Dance of Alabama?

7. Which states border Alabama?

8. Mobile, Alabama claims the first Mardi Gras celebration. What U.S. city now claims the largest Mardi Gras celebration?

9. What is the highest covered bridge over water in the United States?

10. What famous lady is called the "mother of the modern day civil rights movement?"

11. In Huntsville, Alabama you can land a space shuttle, hover over Mars, or rendezvous with Jupiter—all from the comfort of a simulated command module. What is this space center called?

12. What is the name of the "vine that ate the south?"

13. Alabama has had five capital cities. Where were the first four, and what is now the capital?

14. Spanish Moss is not moss and it is not Spanish— what is it?

15. What was the first word Helen Keller finally recognized and where was she?

16. What explorer spent time in Alabama in 1540?

17. What city is Alabama's major seaport?

18. What are Alabama's most valuable agricultural products?

19. In what city can you find the National Voting Rights Museum and Institute?

20. Where did scientist George Washington Carver produce many agricultural discoveries?

Boll Weevil Answers

1. Sequoyah Caverns are the location of beautiful colored formations and looking-glass rim stone pools.

2. Chief Tuscaloosa.

3. "We Dare Maintain Our Rights," which has been on the state coat of arms since 1923.

4. The Tennessee River, where locks were constructed.

5. James Monroe, the fifth President of the United States.

6. The Square Dance.

7. The states of Georgia, Florida, Mississippi and Tennessee.

8. The largest Mardi Gras celebration today is held in New Orleans, Louisiana.

9. Horton Mill Bridge is the highest covered bridge over water in the U.S. It stands 70 ft. over the Warrior River.

10. Rosa Parks refused to give up her seat on a bus in Montgomery, Alabama.

11. U.S. Space and Rocket Center or the George C. Marshall Space Flight Center.

12. Kudzu is the vine that grows up trees and hillsides creating imaginary forms of all shapes.

13. St. Stephens was the first and William Wyatt Bibb was declared governor. Then the site was moved to Huntsville, then Cahaba, then Tuscaloosa and finally Montgomery. The area around the capitol building is called "goat hill" because at one time, goats grazed on the property.

14. Spanish moss is a type of plant that has no roots but lives off moisture in the atmosphere. Their tendrils trap rain and they grow very well on old and decaying trees. The "moss" is sometimes used as packing material and upholstery stuffing.

15. Helen Keller recognized the word water as she stood by her family's water pump with her teacher Anne Sullivan.

16. Hernando DeSoto.

17. Mobile, Alabama is the state's major seaport.

18. Broiler chickens and cattle are the most important agricultural products in Alabama.

19. Selma, Alabama displays a variety of struggles and accomplishments during the voting rights movement.

20. Tuskegee, the home of the Carver Museum and laboratory.

Carol Crane

Y is for Yellowhammer is Carol's tenth book with Sleeping Bear Press. She has authored numerous alphabet books in their Discover America State by State series, from Alaska (*L is for Last Frontier*) to Florida (*S is for Sunshine*) as well as companion counting books including *Sunny Numbers: A Florida Counting Book* and *Round Up: A Texas Numbers Book*. She is widely known for her expertise in children's literature.

Carol is a historian and traveler, and fell in love with Alabama and her people the first time she had a bowl of grits and a catfish dinner in Decatur. She has traveled by boat up the Tennessee River, by car on their many highways, and wishes she could have soared to the moon in a rocket in Huntsville.

Ted Burn

Ted Burn's career as a painter has evolved from 30 years as a graphic designer and 18 years as a successful illustrator. Educated at Presbyterian College and The Art Institute at The High Museum of Art in Atlanta, Ted has also taught classes at the Eastern Shore Arts Association in Fairhope, Alabama.

Ted's hobbies include building small boats, and he sails on one called Water Color. He also has a skiff called Sketch. He is an avid gardener and will soon be moving back to Daphne, Alabama with his wife, Dianne and their numerous pets, including two dogs and four cats.